"Dog Breeds"
Design Book #9

SCROLL SAW
FRETWORK PATTERNS
"Fine Line Design"™

by

Judy Gale Roberts® and *Jerry Booher*

Fretwork: an ornamental design consisting of repeated and often symmetrical figures, open in relief, sometimes contained within a band or border.

A very special thank you, to contributing artist, Marilyn M. Roberts of Houston, Texas

Contents Design Book #9

For extra detail you can shade in the areas indicated by a dashed line (as shown in the illustration on the right). You can either paint or stain this shade. If using stain, use a wood-burner to draw a line (using the dashed lines as a guide) to "break" the grain so the stain will not bleed over to unwanted areas. On many of these dogs it would be a good idea to cut the nose area first. As a general rule cut the most fragile areas first.

41 Shih Tzu

For extra detail you can shade in the areas indicated by a dashed line (as shown in the illustration on the right). You can either paint or stain this shade. If using stain, use a wood-burner to draw a line (using the dashed lines as a guide) to "break" the grain so the stain will not bleed over to unwanted areas. On many of these dogs it would be a good idea to cut the nose area first. As a general rule cut the most fragile areas first.

41 Shih Tzu

Helpful Hints

Listed below are suggestions and helpful ideas that can be used for the projects in this book. Feel free to use whatever materials, sizes, and technique that best suit your needs.

Material list:

1/8 to 1/4" plywood for the fretwork cut outs, or you can use a solid wood of your choosing (mahogany, oak, walnut, etc.). The solid wood should be at least 1/2" thick for added strength.

Method of laying out:

Several methods for the lay out can be used;

Using a photo copier to make copies of the original drawing, use a repositioning adhesive spray applied to the back of the paper and apply the paper pattern to the face of the wood.

Using carbon paper you can carefully re-draw the pattern to transfer the layout lines onto the wood.

Using either method above, carefully make a master template made of thin plywood, cardboard or plastic. Use this template as a master and carefully draw around it, transferring the design to the plywood or material that you are using.

CUT OUT areas marked with the x's:

Circles can be drilled only - just find a drill that most closely matches the diameter of the circle. These areas could also be burned or painted if you do not have the appropriate size drill.

Additional Information:

Depending on material thickness, use double sided tape or staples, stack cut at least two pieces at one time. Cutting four at one time is also feasible.

When your project is complete and assembled, try taping or gluing a colorful fabric to the backside of the fretwork pieces. This can be a solid material or have some sort of pattern on it (perhaps a material that matches your curtains or one to match your table cloth if it is to be used in the kitchen or dinning room). This really adds to the overall effect of the design.

A wood burner may be used to add extra detail, these areas are indicated with a dashed line and are noted on the patterns which call for extra detail .

Many of the patterns could be altered to add a shelf (as shown in the illustration below). All of these designs make nice wall hangings.

NOTE: The single black lines on this design (and many others in this book) are a single blade width cut. The saw blade kerf creates the line work which defines that portion of the fretwork. These areas could be burned if desired.

Shelf

You can extend the lower portion and add a shelf.

NOTE: For extra detail you can shade in the areas indicated by dashed lines on the pattern. You can either paint or stain this shade. If using a stain, use a wood-burner (follow the dashed lines as a guide) to "break" the grain to keep the stain from bleeding to unwanted areas.

For extra detail you can shade in the areas indicated by a dashed line (as shown in the illustration on the right). You can either paint or stain this shade. If using stain, use a wood-burner to draw a line (using the dashed lines as a guide) to "break" the grain so the stain will not bleed over to unwanted areas. On many of these dogs it would be a good idea to cut the nose area first. As a general rule cut the most fragile areas first.

2 Alaskan Malamute

For extra detail you can shade in the areas indicated by a dashed line (as shown in the illustration on the right). You can either paint or stain this shade. If using stain, use a woodburner to draw a line (using the dashed lines as a guide) to "break" the grain so the stain will not bleed over to unwanted areas. On many of these dogs it would be a good idea to cut the nose area first. As a general rule cut the most fragile areas first.

3 American Staffordshire Terrier

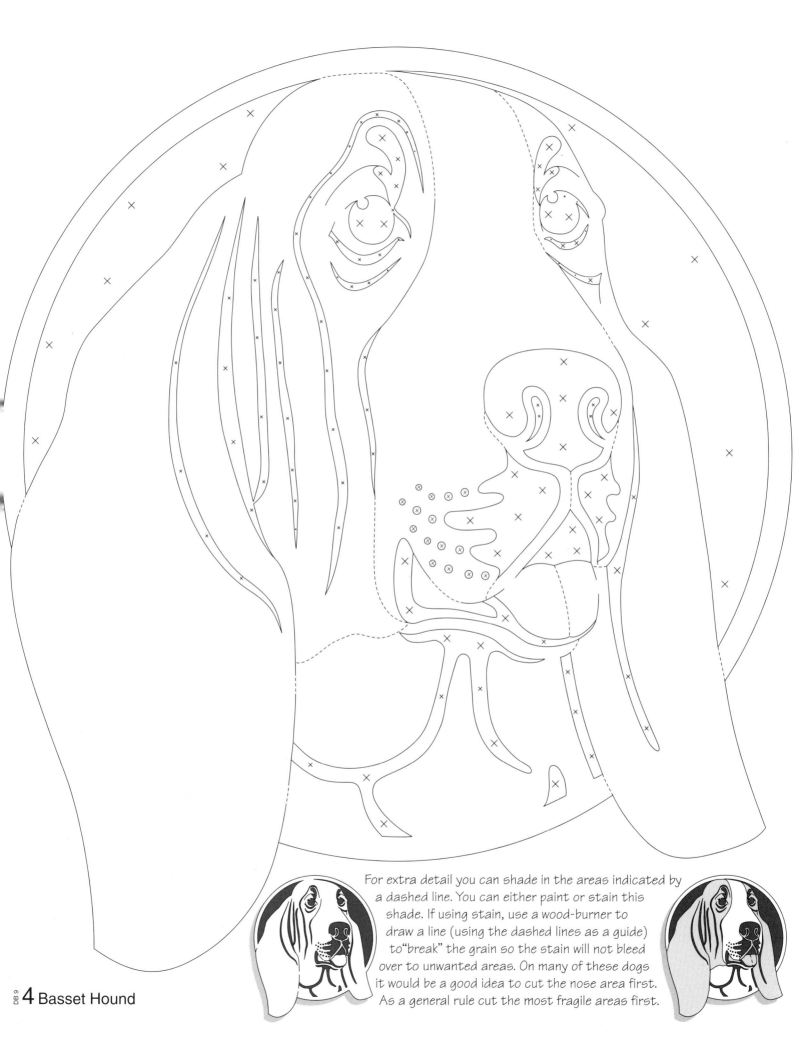

For extra detail you can shade in the areas indicated by a dashed line. You can either paint or stain this shade. If using stain, use a wood-burner to draw a line (using the dashed lines as a guide) to "break" the grain so the stain will not bleed over to unwanted areas. On many of these dogs it would be a good idea to cut the nose area first. As a general rule cut the most fragile areas first.

4 Basset Hound

For extra detail you can shade in the areas indicated by a dashed line (as shown in the illustration on the right). You can either paint or stain this shade. If using stain, use a wood-burner to draw a line (using the dashed lines as a guide) to "break" the grain so the stain will not bleed over to unwanted areas. On many of these dogs it would be a good idea to cut the nose area first. As a general rule cut the most fragile areas first.

For extra detail you can shade in the areas indicated by a dashed line (as shown in the illustration on the right). You can either paint or stain this shade. If using stain, use a wood-burner to draw a line (using the dashed lines as a guide) to "break" the grain so the stain will not bleed over to unwanted areas. On many of these dogs it would be a good idea to cut the nose area first. As a general rule cut the most fragile areas first.

For extra detail you can shade in the areas indicated by a dashed line (as shown in the illustration on the right). You can either paint or stain this shade. If using stain, use a wood-burner to draw a line (using the dashed lines as a guide) to "break" the grain so the stain will not bleed over to unwanted areas. On many of these dogs it would be a good idea to cut the nose area first. As a general rule cut the most fragile areas first.

7 Boston Terrier

For extra detail you can shade in the areas indicated by a dashed line (as shown in the illustration on the right). You can either paint or stain this shade. If using stain, use a wood-burner to draw a line (using the dashed lines as a guide) to "break" the grain so the stain will not bleed over to unwanted areas. On many of these dogs it would be a good idea to cut the nose area first. As a general rule cut the most fragile areas first.

For extra detail you can shade in the areas indicated by a dashed line (as shown in the illustration on the right). You can either paint or stain this shade. If using stain, use a wood-burner to draw a line (using the dashed lines as a guide) to "break" the grain so the stain will not bleed over to unwanted areas. On many of these dogs it would be a good idea to cut the nose area first. As a general rule cut the most fragile areas first.

For extra detail you can shade in the areas indicated by a dashed line (as shown in the illustration on the right). You can either paint or stain this shade. If using stain, use a wood-burner to draw a line (using the dashed lines as a guide) to "break" the grain so the stain will not bleed over to unwanted areas. On many of these dogs it would be a good idea to cut the nose area first. As a general rule cut the most fragile areas first.

For extra detail you can shade in the areas indicated by a dashed line (as shown in the illustration on the right). You can either paint or stain this shade. If using stain, use a wood-burner to draw a line (using the dashed lines as a guide) to "break" the grain so the stain will not bleed over to unwanted areas. On many of these dogs it would be a good idea to cut the nose area first. As a general rule cut the most fragile areas first.

For extra detail you can shade in the areas indicated by a dashed line (as shown in the illustration on the right). You can either paint or stain this shade. If using stain, use a wood-burner to draw a line (using the dashed lines as a guide) to "break" the grain so the stain will not bleed over to unwanted areas. On many of these dogs it would be a good idea to cut the nose area first. As a general rule cut the most fragile areas first.

For extra detail you can shade in the areas indicated by a dashed line (as shown in the illustration on the right). You can either paint or stain this shade. If using stain, use a wood-burner to draw a line (using the dashed lines as a guide) to "break" the grain so the stain will not bleed over to unwanted areas. On many of these dogs it would be a good idea to cut the nose area first. As a general rule cut the most fragile areas first.

For extra detail you can shade in the areas indicated by a dashed line. You can either paint or stain this shade. If using stain, use a wood-burner to draw a line (using the dashed lines as a guide) to "break" the grain so the stain will not bleed over to unwanted areas. On many of these dogs it would be a good idea to cut the nose area first. As a general rule cut the most fragile areas first.

For extra detail you can shade in the areas indicated by a dashed line (as shown in the illustration on the right). You can either paint or stain this shade. If using stain, use a wood-burner to draw a line (using the dashed lines as a guide) to "break" the grain so the stain will not bleed over to unwanted areas. On many of these dogs it would be a good idea to cut the nose area first. As a general rule cut the most fragile areas first.

For extra detail you can shade in the areas indicated by a dashed line (as shown in the illustration on the right). You can either paint or stain this shade. If using stain, use a wood-burner to draw a line (using the dashed lines as a guide) to "break" the grain so the stain will not bleed over to unwanted areas. On many of these dogs it would be a good idea to cut the nose area first. As a general rule cut the most fragile areas first.

For extra detail you can shade in the areas indicated by a dashed line. You can either paint or stain this shade. If using stain, use a wood-burner to draw a line (using the dashed lines as a guide) to "break" the grain so the stain will not bleed over to unwanted areas. On many of these dogs it would be a good idea to cut the nose area first. As a general rule cut the most fragile areas first.

For extra detail you can shade in the areas indicated by a dashed line (as shown in the illustration on the right). You can either paint or stain this shade. If using stain, use a wood-burner to draw a line (using the dashed lines as a guide) to "break" the grain so the stain will not bleed over to unwanted areas. On many of these dogs it would be a good idea to cut the nose area first. As a general rule cut the most fragile areas first.

For extra detail you can shade in the areas indicated by a dashed line (as shown in the illustration on the right). You can either paint or stain this shade. If using stain, use a wood-burner to draw a line (using the dashed lines as a guide) to "break" the grain so the stain will not bleed over to unwanted areas. On many of these dogs it would be a good idea to cut the nose area first. As a general rule cut the most fragile areas first.

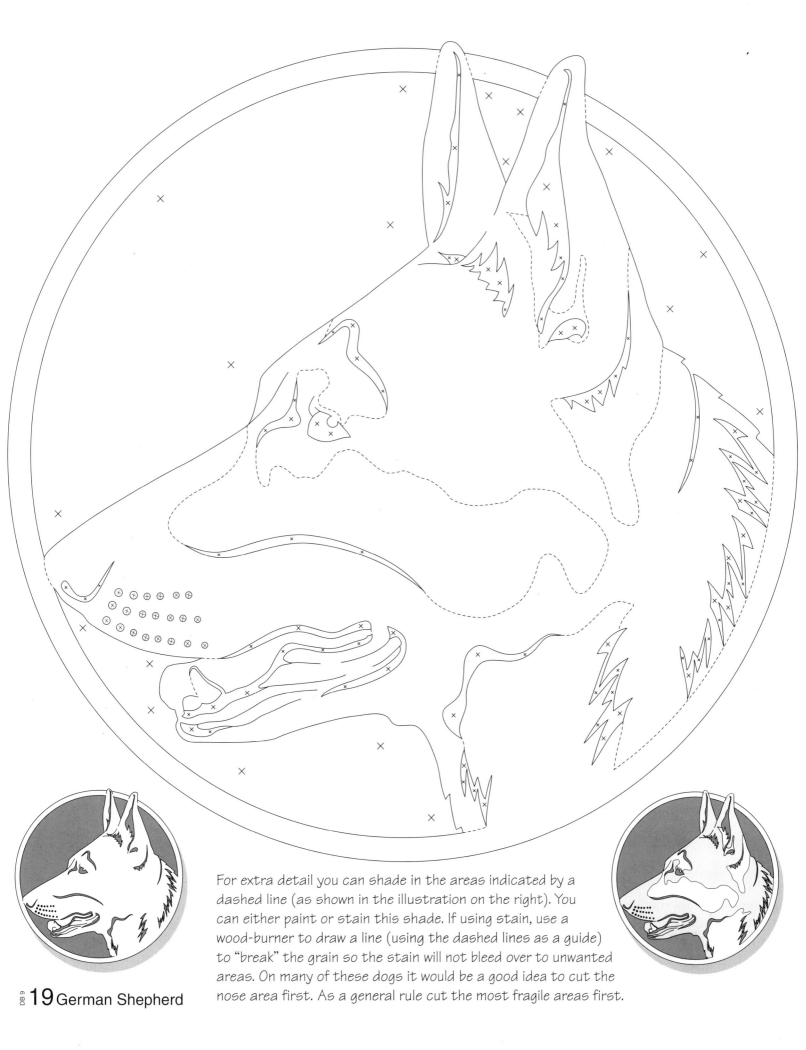

For extra detail you can shade in the areas indicated by a dashed line (as shown in the illustration on the right). You can either paint or stain this shade. If using stain, use a wood-burner to draw a line (using the dashed lines as a guide) to "break" the grain so the stain will not bleed over to unwanted areas. On many of these dogs it would be a good idea to cut the nose area first. As a general rule cut the most fragile areas first.

19 German Shepherd

For extra detail you can shade in the areas indicated by a dashed line (as shown in the illustration on the right). You can either paint or stain this shade. If using stain, use a wood-burner to draw a line (using the dashed lines as a guide) to "break" the grain so the stain will not bleed over to unwanted areas. On many of these dogs it would be a good idea to cut the nose area first. As a general rule cut the most fragile areas first.

For extra detail you can shade in the areas indicated by a dashed line (as shown in the illustration on the right). You can either paint or stain this shade. If using stain, use a wood-burner to draw a line (using the dashed lines as a guide) to "break" the grain so the stain will not bleed over to unwanted areas. On many of these dogs it would be a good idea to cut the nose area first. As a general rule cut the most fragile areas first.

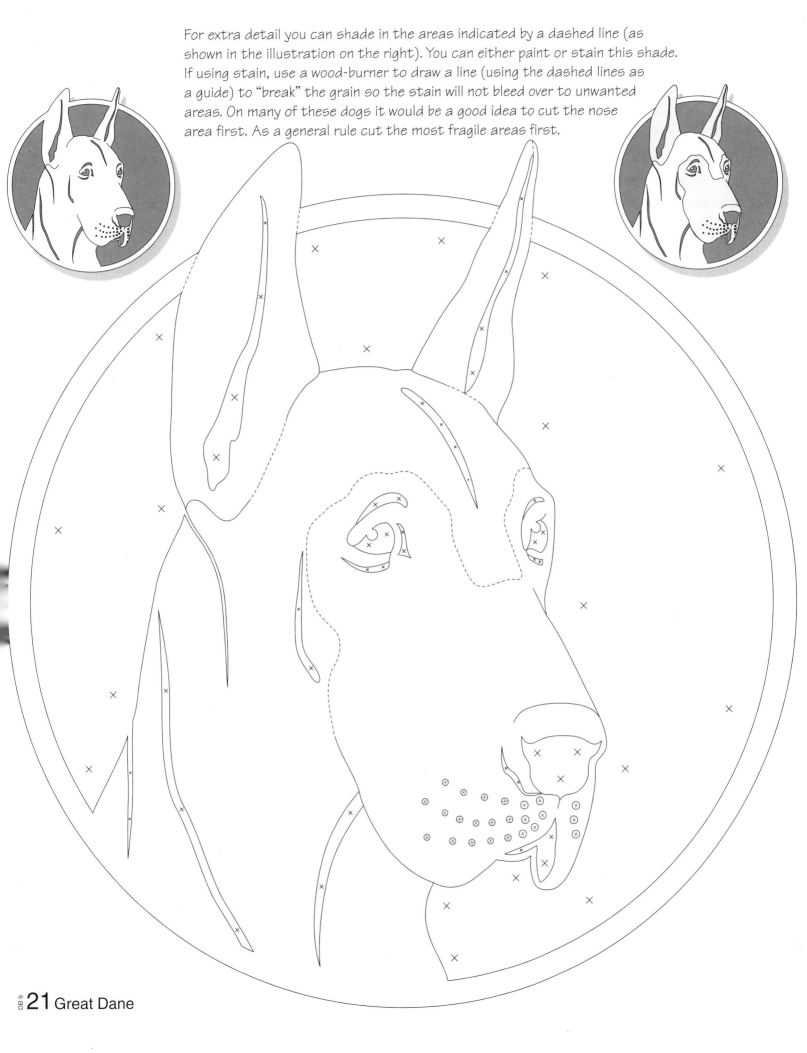

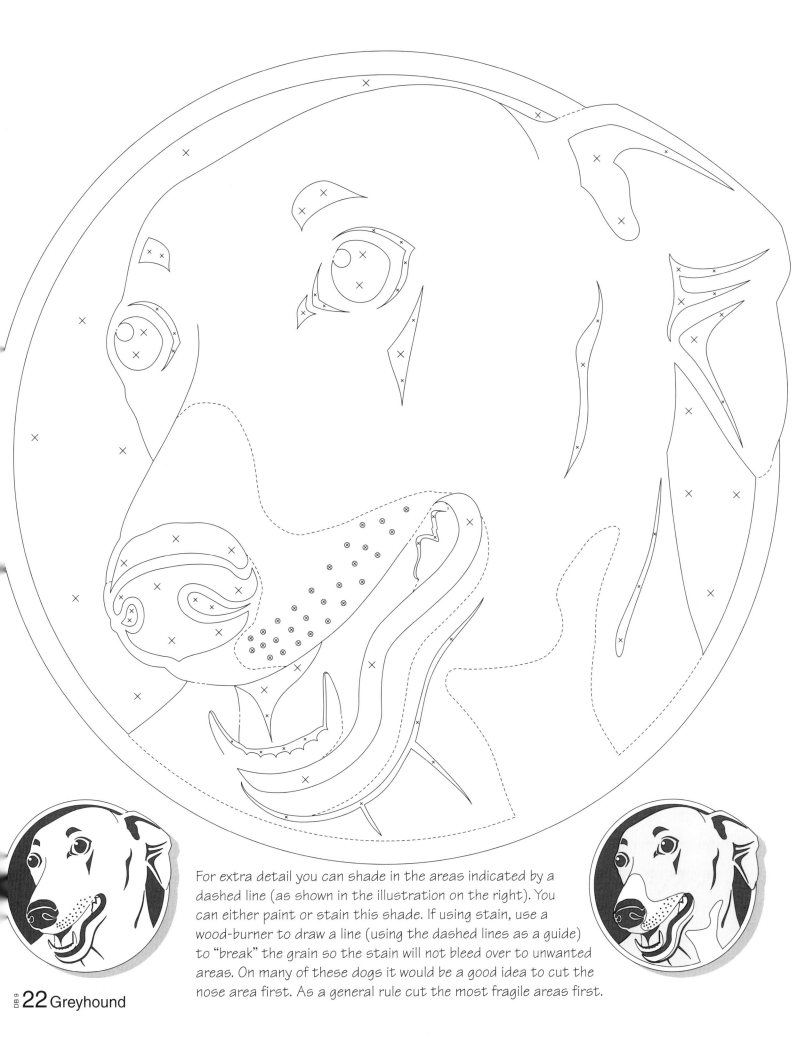

For extra detail you can shade in the areas indicated by a dashed line (as shown in the illustration on the right). You can either paint or stain this shade. If using stain, use a wood-burner to draw a line (using the dashed lines as a guide) to "break" the grain so the stain will not bleed over to unwanted areas. On many of these dogs it would be a good idea to cut the nose area first. As a general rule cut the most fragile areas first.

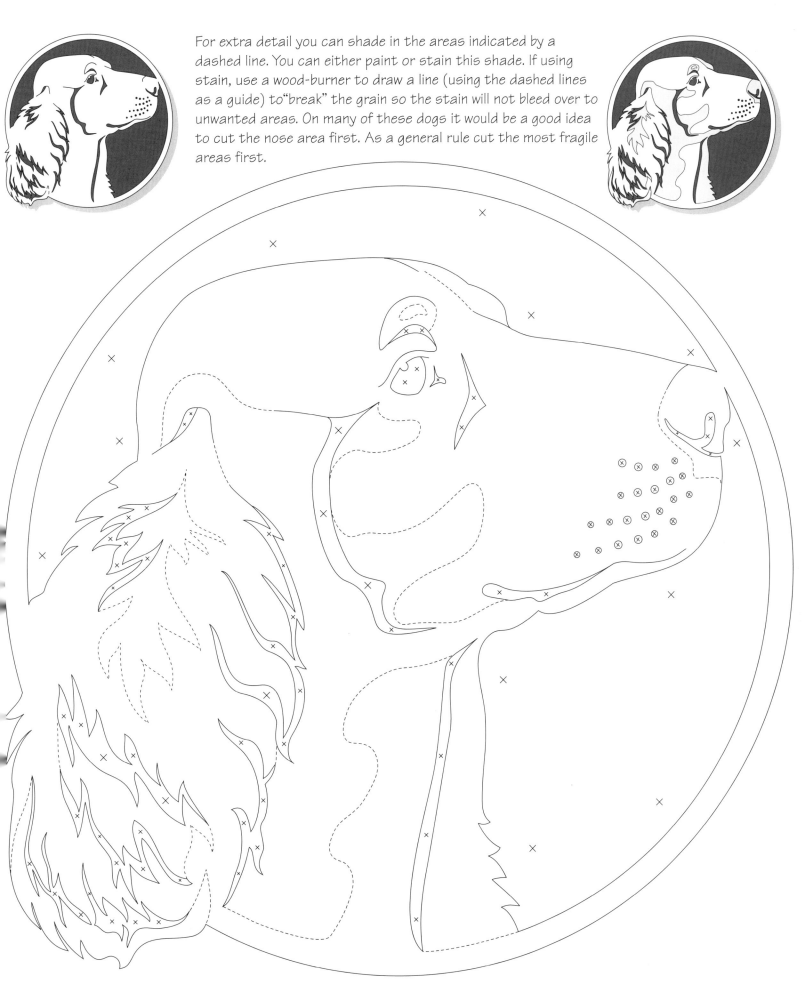

For extra detail you can shade in the areas indicated by a dashed line. You can either paint or stain this shade. If using stain, use a wood-burner to draw a line (using the dashed lines as a guide) to "break" the grain so the stain will not bleed over to unwanted areas. On many of these dogs it would be a good idea to cut the nose area first. As a general rule cut the most fragile areas first.

For extra detail you can shade in the areas indicated by a dashed line (as shown in the illustration on the right). You can either paint or stain this shade. If using stain, use a wood-burner to draw a line (using the dashed lines as a guide) to "break" the grain so the stain will not bleed over to unwanted areas. On many of these dogs it would be a good idea to cut the nose area first. As a general rule cut the most fragile areas first.

For extra detail you can shade in the areas indicated by a dashed line (as shown in the illustration on the right). You can either paint or stain this shade. If using stain, use a wood-burner to draw a line (using the dashed lines as a guide) to "break" the grain so the stain will not bleed over to unwanted areas. On many of these dogs it would be a good idea to cut the nose area first. As a general rule cut the most fragile areas first.

For extra detail you can shade in the areas indicated by a dashed line (as shown in the illustration on the right). You can either paint or stain this shade. If using stain, use a wood-burner to draw a line (using the dashed lines as a guide) to "break" the grain so the stain will not bleed over to unwanted areas. On many of these dogs it would be a good idea to cut the nose area first. As a general rule cut the most fragile areas first.

For extra detail you can shade in the areas indicated by a dashed line (as shown in the illustration on the right). You can either paint or stain this shade. If using stain, use a wood-burner to draw a line (using the dashed lines as a guide) to "break" the grain so the stain will not bleed over to unwanted areas. On many of these dogs it would be a good idea to cut the nose area first. As a general rule cut the most fragile areas first.

The Mongrel would look great cut from either a light shade to a dark shade of wood (or plywood veneers).
On many of these dogs it would be a good idea to cut the nose area first. As a general rule cut the most fragile areas first.

For extra detail you can shade in the areas indicated by a dashed line (as shown in the illustration on the right). You can either paint or stain this shade. If using stain, use a wood-burner to draw a line (using the dashed lines as a guide) to "break" the grain so the stain will not bleed over to unwanted areas. On many of these dogs it would be a good idea to cut the nose area first. As a general rule cut the most fragile areas first.

For extra detail you can shade in the areas indicated by a dashed line (as shown in the illustration on the right). You can either paint or stain this shade. If using stain, use a woodburner to draw a line (using the dashed lines as a guide) to "break" the grain so the stain will not bleed over to unwanted areas. On many of these dogs it would be a good idea to cut the nose area first. As a general rule cut the most fragile areas first.

On many of these dogs it would be a good idea to cut the nose area first. As a general rule cut the most fragile areas first.

The poodle would look great cut from either a light shade to a dark shade of wood (or plywood veneers).
On many of these dogs it would be a good idea to cut the nose area first. As a general rule cut the most fragile areas first.

For extra detail you can shade in the areas indicated by a dashed line (as shown in the illustration on the right). You can either paint or stain this shade. If using stain, use a wood-burner to draw a line (using the dashed lines as a guide) to "break" the grain so the stain will not bleed over to unwanted areas. On many of these dogs it would be a good idea to cut the nose area first. As a general rule cut the most fragile areas first.

For extra detail you can shade in the areas indicated by a dashed line (as shown in the illustration on the right). You can either paint or stain this shade. If using stain, use a wood-burner to draw a line (using the dashed lines as a guide) to "break" the grain so the stain will not bleed over to unwanted areas. On many of these dogs it would be a good idea to cut the nose area first. As a general rule cut the most fragile areas first.

For extra detail you can shade in the areas indicated by a dashed line (as shown in the illustration on the right). You can either paint or stain this shade. If using stain, use a wood-burner to draw a line (using the dashed lines as a guide) to "break" the grain so the stain will not bleed over to unwanted areas. On many of these dogs it would be a good idea to cut the nose area first. As a general rule cut the most fragile areas first.

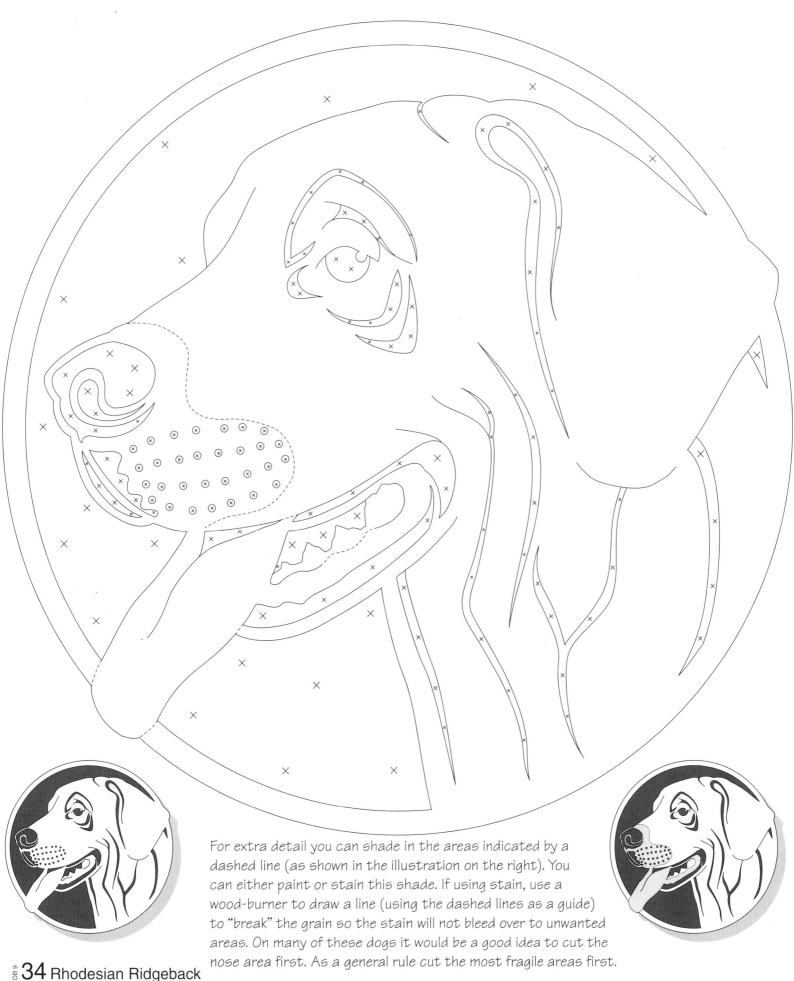

For extra detail you can shade in the areas indicated by a dashed line (as shown in the illustration on the right). You can either paint or stain this shade. If using stain, use a wood-burner to draw a line (using the dashed lines as a guide) to "break" the grain so the stain will not bleed over to unwanted areas. On many of these dogs it would be a good idea to cut the nose area first. As a general rule cut the most fragile areas first.

For extra detail you can shade in the areas indicated by a dashed line (as shown in the illustration on the right). You can either paint or stain this shade. If using stain, use a wood-burner to draw a line (using the dashed lines as a guide) to "break" the grain so the stain will not bleed over to unwanted areas. On many of these dogs it would be a good idea to cut the nose area first. As a general rule cut the most fragile areas first.

DB 9 **35** Rotweiler

For extra detail you can shade in the areas indicated by a dashed line (as shown in the illustration on the right). You can either paint or stain this shade. If using stain, use a wood-burner to draw a line (using the dashed lines as a guide) to "break" the grain so the stain will not bleed over to unwanted areas. On many of these dogs it would be a good idea to cut the nose area first. As a general rule cut the most fragile areas first.

For extra detail you can shade in the areas indicated by a dashed line. You can either paint or stain this shade. If using stain, use a wood-burner to draw a line (using the dashed lines as a guide) to "break" the grain so the stain will not bleed over to unwanted areas. On many of these dogs it would be a good idea to cut the nose area first. As a general rule cut the most fragile areas first.

For extra detail you can shade in the areas indicated by a dashed line. You can either paint or stain this shade. If using stain, use a wood-burner to draw a line (using the dashed lines as a guide) to "break" the grain so the stain will not bleed over to unwanted areas. On many of these dogs it would be a good idea to cut the nose area first. As a general rule cut the most fragile areas first.

For extra detail you can shade in the areas indicated by a dashed line. You can either paint or stain this shade. If using stain, use a wood-burner to draw a line (using the dashed lines as a guide) to"break" the grain so the stain will not bleed over to unwanted areas. On many of these dogs it would be a good idea to cut the nose area first. As a general rule cut the most fragile areas first.

For extra detail you can shade in the areas indicated by a dashed line (as shown in the illustration on the right). You can either paint or stain this shade. If using stain, use a wood-burner to draw a line (using the dashed lines as a guide) to "break" the grain so the stain will not bleed over to unwanted areas. On many of these dogs it would be a good idea to cut the nose area first. As a general rule cut the most fragile areas first.

For extra detail you can shade in the areas indicated by a
dashed line (as shown in the illustration on the right). You
can either paint or stain this shade. If using stain, use a
wood-burner to draw a line (using the dashed lines as a guide)
to "break" the grain so the stain will not bleed over to unwanted
areas. On many of these dogs it would be a good idea to cut the
nose area first. As a general rule cut the most fragile areas first.

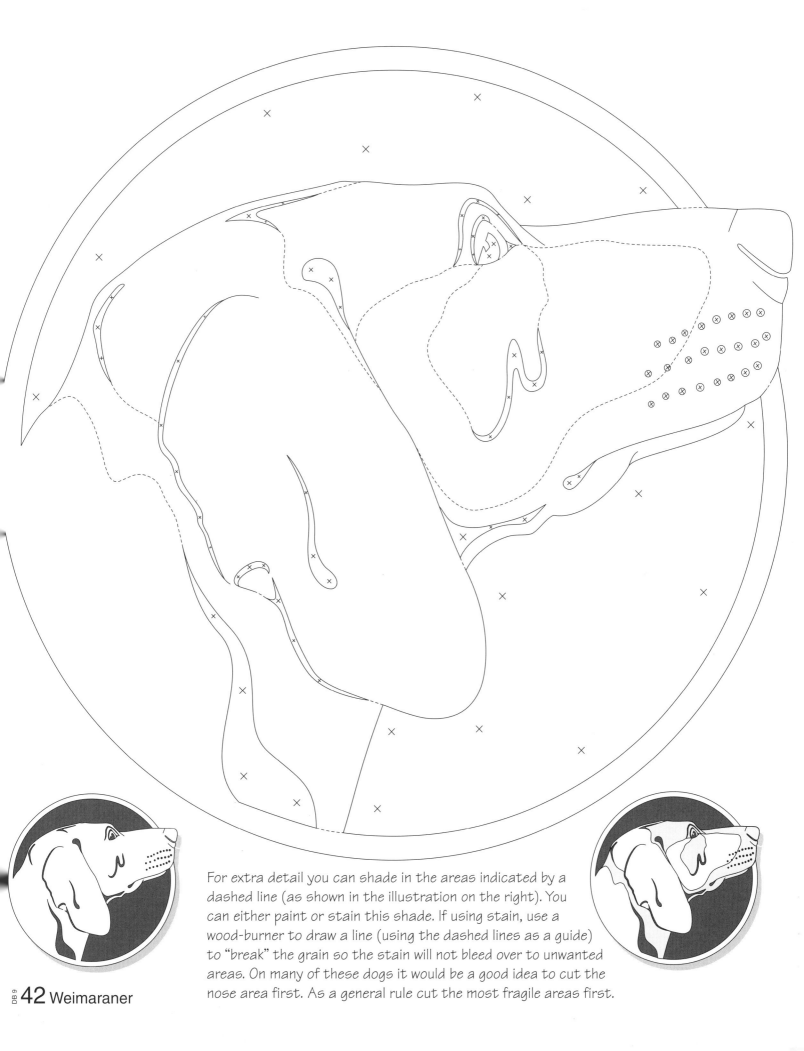

For extra detail you can shade in the areas indicated by a dashed line (as shown in the illustration on the right). You can either paint or stain this shade. If using stain, use a wood-burner to draw a line (using the dashed lines as a guide) to "break" the grain so the stain will not bleed over to unwanted areas. On many of these dogs it would be a good idea to cut the nose area first. As a general rule cut the most fragile areas first.

For extra detail you can shade in the areas indicated by a dashed line (as shown in the illustration on the right). You can either paint or stain this shade. If using stain, use a wood-burner to draw a line (using the dashed lines as a guide) to "break" the grain so the stain will not bleed over to unwanted areas. On many of these dogs it would be a good idea to cut the nose area first. As a general rule cut the most fragile areas first.

43 Welsh Corgis

For extra detail you can shade in the areas indicated by a dashed line (as shown in the illustration on the right). You can either paint or stain this shade. If using stain, use a wood-burner to draw a line (using the dashed lines as a guide) to "break" the grain so the stain will not bleed over to unwanted areas. On many of these dogs it would be a good idea to cut the nose area first. As a general rule cut the most fragile areas first.

For extra detail you can shade in the areas indicated by a dashed line (as shown in the illustration on the right). You can either paint or stain this shade. If using stain, use a wood-burner to draw a line (using the dashed lines as a guide) to "break" the grain so the stain will not bleed over to unwanted areas. On many of these dogs it would be a good idea to cut the nose area first. As a general rule cut the most fragile areas first.

45 Wire Fox Terrier

For extra detail you can shade in the areas indicated by a dashed line (as shown in the illustration on the right). You can either paint or stain this shade. If using stain, use a wood-burner to draw a line (using the dashed lines as a guide) to "break" the grain so the stain will not bleed over to unwanted areas. On many of these dogs it would be a good idea to cut the nose area first. As a general rule cut the most fragile areas first.